PROJECT 2025 EXPLAINED IN SIMPLE TERMS

**Understanding The Proposed Mandate For
Conservative Government**

JR Grant

This book is dedicated to all Americans who strive for a better tomorrow

Contents

Introduction

So, "Project 2025," which is also known as the "Presidential Transition Project," is this batch of ideas coming from the Heritage Foundation. They're leaning pretty conservative and right-wing, and the whole idea is to shake up the U.S. federal government and ramp up the president's power if the Republicans snag the 2024 election. One of the main moves would be to switch a lot of federal jobs over to political appointments so they can bring in people who really back the next Republican president's game plan. Plus, they want to really weave Christian values into the fabric of government and society.

Those in favor of Project 2025 talk about it like it's a fix to cut down a huge, unchecked government bureaucracy. But on the flip side, the critics are saying it's got shades of authoritarian Christian nationalism and might push the U.S. towards being more like an autocracy. A bunch of legal experts are weighing in too, warning that it could mess with the rule of law, blur the lines between the different branches of government, mix government too much with religion, and step on a whole range of civil liberties, affecting everyone from women and racial minorities to the LGBTQ community.

Project 2025 is all about shaking things up in the federal government, especially when it comes to economic and social policies, and how government agencies are structured. They want to put partisan control over major agencies like the Department of Justice, FBI, Department of Commerce, FCC, and FTC. The plan even suggests getting rid of the Department of Homeland Security and slashing regulations on environmental and climate issues to boost fossil fuel production.

Economically speaking, Project 2025 is pushing for tax cuts. There seems to be some back-and-forth among the folks behind the plan about protectionist policies. They're also talking about scrapping the

Department of Education altogether, either moving its programs to other agencies or cutting them off completely. Funding for climate research would take a hit, and they want to reshape the NIH to follow more conservative principles.

The project also wants to cut back on funding for Medicare and Medicaid and is pretty clear about saying no to abortion as a form of health care. According to the plan, life starts at conception, and they want to stop coverage for emergency contraception under the Affordable Care Act. They're also keen on using the Comstock Act to go after anyone sending or receiving contraceptives and abortion pills across the country.

In a nutshell, Project 2025 aims to totally redo what the federal government does and how it does it, all steering towards more conservative and Christian nationalist values. Project 2025 is all about bringing Christian ideals and principles into both government and society. The plan includes some pretty controversial stuff, like making pornography illegal and getting rid of laws that protect against discrimination based on sexual orientation and gender identity. It also wants to shut down diversity, equity, and inclusion programs, along with affirmative action, and it even suggests that the DOJ should go after what it calls 'anti-white racism.'

Moreover, the project has some drastic ideas for dealing with undocumented immigrants in the U.S. It talks about using the military to capture and detain them in international camps. They're considering using the Insurrection Act of 1807, which would allow the military to help with domestic policing and to round up undocumented immigrants.

When it comes to the criminal justice system, Project 2025 pushes for more capital punishment and wants these death sentences carried out quickly. It also sees a role for the military in everyday law enforcement. Basically, Project 2025 is a deep dive into reshaping our government and society through a pretty heavy Christian nationalist lens. It's focused on changing how we handle social and cultural issues, immigration, criminal justice, and even the role of the military right here at home. Project 2025 has ruffled some feathers, even among some conservatives and Republicans, especially with its take on climate change and foreign trade. Others criticize the project as more of a cover for what could be a four-year rampage of personal revenge, costs be damned.

The folks behind Project 2025 know that to get most of their ideas through, they'd need the Republican Party to hold both the House and the Senate. Plus, some parts of their plan have already been knocked down by the Supreme Court as unconstitutional and would probably get tied up in legal battles. However, some of the more boundary-pushing suggestions might just make it through the courts.

Legally, Project 2025 can't back a particular presidential candidate, but it's no secret that many involved have close connections to former President Donald Trump and his 2024 campaign run. The Washington Post even called it a detailed preview of what we might expect from a second Trump term. John McEntee, from the Trump campaign, mentioned in April 2024 that they were looking to weave a lot of Project 2025's ideas into their campaign efforts by summer.

In a nutshell, from internal skepticism to legal issues and political implications, Project 2025 has sparked a broad spectrum of criticism and raised concerns that stretch from constitutional worries all the way to its apparent ties with the Trump campaign's 2024 run.

You know, at first the Trump campaign was actually pretty into Project 2025 - they thought it lined up well with their own Agenda 47 plans. But lately, it seems like the project has been causing some major headaches for the campaign. They've been trying to avoid getting too specific on policy proposals that could come back to haunt Trump, you know?

Then in July 2024, Trump himself came out and said he had no idea what Project 2025 even was and wanted nothing to do with it. Which is kinda weird, right? Because a bunch of his top advisors and former administration officials were the ones who helped put the whole thing together in the first place. They were totally on board with it.

My guess is the Trump team realized Project 2025 had some ideas that were just too extreme and controversial. Stuff that could really hurt Trump's chances of getting reelected if he's not careful. Even though the project started out as an inside job with his closest allies, now they're trying to put some distance between Trump and the crazier parts of the plan.

It's a tricky balancing act - Trump wants to keep his hardcore supporters happy with the bold ideas, but he also needs to win over some moderates and independents to pull off a victory. Disavowing Project 2025 is probably a strategic move to clean up his image a bit without totally abandoning the principles. We'll have to see if it works out for him in the end.

Background History of Project 2025

The Heritage Foundation, a notable conservative think tank, has been rolling out its Mandate for Leadership series every presidential election cycle since 1981. They really think of it as a kind of "policy bible" that lays out a roadmap for new administrations.

Kevin Roberts, the current president of the Heritage Foundation, has made it clear that they're aiming to "institutionalize Trumpism," which is all about embedding the politics and policies we saw during former President Trump's time in office. Building on that goal, Roberts kicked off Project 2021 on April 21, 2023, aiming to arm the 2024 Republican presidential nominee with not just a full roster of people but also a solid ideological framework to guide them.

The push to start Project 2025 didn't just come out of the blue. It was really sparked by several events during the Trump era, like when civil servants pushed back against moves like the Muslim travel ban, or the drama over trying to appoint a new attorney general to challenge the 2020 election results, not to mention Trump's controversial stance on using lethal force during the George Floyd protests.

Spencer Chretien, the associate project director, has been quite upfront about the project's purpose. He's said, "It was past time to lay the groundwork for a White House that's more receptive to right-leaning ideas." Essentially, Project 2025 is all about setting the stage for the next Republican administration, shaping both the people who will lead and the policies they'll push.

In April 2023, the Heritage Foundation dropped a hefty 920-page policy playbook called the Mandate, penned by a whole bunch of conservative thinkers, including a good number who were part of the Trump administration. It's not just any policy guide;

this one's got the muscle of nearly half its partner organizations funded by so-called "dark money" — basically, cash from donors who don't have to reveal their identities. These funds have links to Leonard Leo, a pretty prominent figure who had a major hand in picking judicial nominees during Trump's tenure.

The fact that so many folks from the Trump era were involved in putting together the Mandate, along with all this financial support coming from Leo's network, really shows that Project 2025 is kind of a continuation of that administration's ideas and the interests of its powerful supporters. This raises some eyebrows, making people wonder about the influence these shadowy funding sources might have on what's being pushed in the Mandate and Project 2025. After all, these are documents that aim to steer the direction of the next Republican government.

Axios reports that while the Heritage Foundation has filled in other Republican candidates about Project 2025, it's really seen as a Trump-centric effort. This vibe largely comes from Johnny McEntee playing a key part in it. McEntee, known as Trump's go-to guy for ensuring loyalty within his circle, serves as a senior advisor for the project.

The Trump 2024 campaign has made it clear that it speaks for itself and that its own "Agenda 47" is the official blueprint for a possible second term. Despite this, after some top Trump campaign officials tried to put some daylight between the campaign and various outside groups, their statement didn't exactly reject these groups. Instead, it seemed more about keeping them from chatting with the media. The campaign did mention, though, that it values input from groups that share its vision.

It's interesting to note that Project 2025 isn't the only conservative effort stocking up a talent pool for a potential future Republican administration, but all these initiatives seem to circle back to Trump. Generally, these efforts aim to ensure that if Trump gets another shot at the presidency, he won't face the same prep issues he had when he first took office.

All these points hint at a broader strategy among conservative circles and Trump's allies to line up the policies and players for a possible second Trump stint in the White House—regardless of the campaign's public stance to maintain some distance from these external influences.

Following an Axios report suggesting that Trump plans to fill a potential second administration with die-hard "MAGA" supporters, anti-establishment characters, and individuals keen to push presidential powers to the limit—including targeting and possibly imprisoning critics from the government and media—the Trump campaign quickly put out a memo trying to distance itself from these claims.

The report also named specific folks being eyed for top spots in a potential second Trump presidency, like Kash Patel, Steve Bannon, and Mike Davis—a former aide to Senator Chuck Grassley who promised a "three-week reign of terror" if he became acting attorney general. Just two days before this, Patel appeared on Bannon's podcast, saying they planned to "go out and find the conspirators—not just in government, but in the media... We're going to come after you. Whether it's criminally or civilly, we'll figure that out."

In June 2024, Bannon even singled out certain current and former FBI and DOJ officials, claiming they'd be pursued for alleged crimes and treason, even if they fled the country.

All this points to a worrying possible turn, with government power being used to target and punish perceived political foes, a step up from usual political rivalry. The distancing efforts by the Trump campaign did little to calm concerns about the kinds of agendas and personalities being lined up for another Trump-led term.

The Key People Behind Project 2025

When Project 2025 kicked off, it brought together a pretty broad mix of over 80 conservative groups, mostly think tanks, along with some universities and The American Conservative magazine. By February 2024, that number had grown to over 100 partnering organizations.

This project has ties to more than 200 former folks from the Trump administration. Some big names contributing to their Mandate for Leadership include Jonathan Berry, Ben Carson, and Ken Cuccinelli among others like Peter Navarro and Paul Winfree. Initially, in November 2023, the Trump campaign kind of brushed off Project 2025, calling it just some "policy recommendations from external allies." But then in July 2024, after a potentially violent remark made by Kevin Roberts, Trump completely disowned the project, claiming he had no clue about it and didn't know who was running the show. However, a lot of pundits like Robert Reich and Michael Steele were pretty skeptical of Trump's sudden denial. The Washington Post even noted that there was regular back-and-forth between Project 2025 and Trump's campaign advisors. Philip Bump from The Washington Post went as far as to say that you can't really separate the Trump Campaign from Project 2025.

Then, in May 2024, Russell Vought was appointed as the policy director for the Republican National Committee's platform committee. Also, back at the 2023 Iowa State Fair, leaders from Project 2025 started scouting out people for potential roles in the government, gearing up for a possible Republican win.

The Proposed Policies Of The Project 2025

Project 2025's key document, the "Mandate for Leadership: The Conservative Promise," sets out four main goals: re-centering the family as the cornerstone of American life, tearing down the bulky administrative state, protecting the nation's sovereignty and borders, and ensuring that individuals can exercise their God-given rights to live freely.

In the foreword, Kevin Roberts, who heads the Heritage Foundation, pulls no punches. He says, "The long march of cultural Marxism through our institutions has come to pass. The federal government has grown into a massive beast, turned against American citizens and conservative values, with our freedoms and liberties under attack like never before." Roberts takes a unique spin on the "pursuit of happiness" from the Declaration of Independence, interpreting it as the "pursuit of blessedness." According to him, this means that "an individual must be free to live as his creator intended—to flourish." He also points out that the U.S. Constitution doesn't just let us do whatever we want; it gives us the freedom to do what we ought to do.

Kevin Roberts believes that the essence of a good life really boils down to family—think marriage, kids, Thanksgiving dinners—and, most importantly, staying rooted in religious devotion and spirituality. He's pretty vocal about his view that by 2024, the U.S. is going through tough times, with families being hit hard by inflation, a rise in drug overdose deaths, and what he describes as the troubling introduction of topics like transgenderism, drag queens, and pornography into school libraries. He's also spoken out about the widespread issue of crime across the country.

The guy steering Project 2025 is Paul Dans, who was the chief of staff at the Office of Personnel

Management under Trump, with Spencer Chretien, a former special assistant to Trump, as his right-hand man. Dans, who's also editing the project's main guide, says Project 2025 rests on four key pillars:

- Their main text, a 30-chapter, 920-page tome called "Mandate for Leadership: The Conservative Promise," aims to lay out a unified vision for managing federal agencies.
- They're putting together a personnel database, open for public contributions, to be shared with the incoming president's team.
- They've launched an online training hub named the Presidential Administration Academy.
- They're prepping a transition playbook to get agency teams ready the moment the new president is sworn in.

While legally Project 2025 can't outright support Trump, his campaign speeches carry a lot of the same themes. He's talked about axing "radical

Marxist prosecutors destroying America," wiping out the "Deep State," and appointing a special prosecutor to target Joe Biden and his family.

Getting into the "Presidential Personnel Database" isn't just a show-up and get-in kind of deal. Candidates have to answer prompts about their beliefs, like naming a public policy figure they admire and why. Their social media will be combed through too. Russell Vought, another project contributor, explained to The Economist the importance of understanding government from an "America First," populist angle, to govern both credibly and effectively.

Policy On U.S Census

Project 2025 is looking to bring back a move from the Trump era to add a citizenship question to the U.S. census, which happens every ten years. Remember, the census isn't just for counting folks—it also determines how to divide up seats in Congress and shape the Electoral College.

The Trump team initially said they wanted this question added to help avoid racial and language discrimination under the Voting Rights Act. However, the Supreme Court wasn't buying it for the 2020 census. They turned down the argument. Also, according to the Fourteenth Amendment of the U.S. Constitution, the numbers used to figure out congressional representation should include everyone living in each state, not just the citizens.

The Project's Proposed Policy On Christian Nationalism

Russell Vought, a key player in Project 2025 and leader of the Center for Renewing America, is pushing hard to weave Christian nationalism into the government and public life, especially if Trump secures a second term. In a 2021 op-ed, Vought championed the idea of Christian nationalism by describing it as acknowledging America's roots as a Christian nation. He argued for keeping institutional separation between church and state intact, but not shutting out Christianity's influence on government and society. He's vocal about his belief that Christians are facing attacks, and he's used his regular meetings with Trump to try to make Christian nationalism a key issue in Trump's potential second term.

Vought's allies include other figures like Christian nationalist William Wolfe, who's all in on setting up a government system based squarely on biblical principles, where "Christ-ordained civil magistrates" would have authority over the American people.

Also in the loop is Brad Onishi, a former Christian nationalist turned academic who studies religion and extremism. He pointed out that Lance Wallnau of the New Apostolic Reformation, who's expressed that Trump was "anointed," announced a partnership with Charlie Kirk from Project 2025. On top of that, the current Speaker of the House, Mike Johnson, has direct connections to the New Apostolic Reformation.

Throughout his 2024 campaign speeches, Trump has been hitting on themes from Project 2025, including bits that push the envelope on promoting Christian nationalism.

Project 2025 Policy On Climate Change

Project 2025 really wants to take a future Republican president way beyond just canceling Biden's climate change executive orders. They're talking about completely ditching efforts to cut down greenhouse gas emissions by proposing things like scrapping regulations that limit emissions, shrinking the Environmental Protection Agency (EPA), and even getting rid of the National Oceanic and Atmospheric Administration (NOAA), which they label as a major player in the "climate change alarm industry."

The plan specifically suggests shutting down the EPA's Office of Environmental Justice and External Civil Rights. It also recommends picking EPA staff—including the science advisor—based on their management skills, not their expertise in science. They want to stop states like California from setting their own tougher car emission rules and to loosen up regulations on the fossil fuel sector, including lifting restrictions on oil drilling set by the Bureau of Land Extent.

Despite warnings from climatologists about the dangers of increased methane leaks, Project 2025's blueprint advocates for greater natural gas use. They're also pushing to repeal the Inflation Reduction Act, which dedicates $370 billion to clean tech, close down various clean energy offices within the Department of Energy, remove climate change tasks from the National Security Council's list of priorities, and even encourage allied countries to rely more on fossil fuels.

Their blueprint boldly states that the U.S. government has a duty to massively develop oil, gas, and coal resources and supports drilling in the Arctic. It suggests blocking the expansion of the national power grid and stifling the shift to renewable energy sources.

While Mandy Gunasekara, a project contributor, admits that human-made climate change is a real thing, she believes it has been politicized and exaggerated. Meanwhile, Project director Paul Dans concedes that climate change is real but isn't convinced that human actions are the cause.

Project 2025 wants to throw out a 2009 EPA finding that declared carbon dioxide emissions harmful to human health, which would stop the federal government from regulating greenhouse gases. They're even suggesting incentives for everyday folks to point out what they see as scientific errors and misconduct in climate research and to challenge climatology findings in court.

The climate section of the report was penned by several authors, including Mandy Gunasekara, a former EPA chief of staff who played a significant role in pulling the U.S. out of the Paris Agreement back in 2017. Bernard McNamee, a lawyer who's worked with various fossil fuel companies, wrote up what the EPA's role should be according to Project 2025. Notably, four of the top authors tied to the report have been vocal in their denial of climate change.

McNamee has brushed off efforts to mitigate climate change, labeling them as merely "progressive" policies. Meanwhile, there's some pushback from within the Republican ranks. Sarah

Hunt, head of the Joseph Rainey Center for Public Policy, has spoken out about the importance of the Inflation Reduction Act, and Utah Representative John Curtis has emphasized the need for Republicans to support solid energy and climate policies. Benji Backer, who founded the American Conservation Coalition, has highlighted a shift among younger Republicans who acknowledge that human activities are impacting the climate and has criticized Project 2025's stance as misguided.

Project 2025 Policy on the Economy

Project 2025 puts forward a bunch of bold ideas for shaking up the economy, some of which are pretty radical in nature. They're not fans of the Federal Reserve at all, suggesting we should just get rid of it because they think it's responsible for the ups and downs in the business cycle. The plan leans towards either free banking or backing currency with something tangible, like gold.

On taxes, they want to keep the Tax Cuts and Jobs Act of 2017 going and simplify personal income taxes down to just two brackets—15% and 30%, with the higher rate kicking in above the Social Security Wage Base. Corporate taxes would drop to 18%, which they argue is currently the most harmful tax. Capital gains and dividends would get a fixed tax rate of 15%, which is a stark contrast to the Biden administration's proposed 45%.

After these tax reforms are in place, Project 2025 suggests making it tougher to undo these changes by requiring a three-fifths majority in Congress to pass any legislation that raises individual or corporate taxes, trying to put what they call a "wall of protection" around their reforms. That said, most people agree that you can't really make laws that bind future Congresses, which is viewed as unconstitutional.

The project also has its sights on either scrapping the Economic Development Administration (EDA) at the Department of Commerce or pivoting it to help rural communities they believe were harmed by the Biden administration's energy policies. They're also interested in boosting the civilian nuclear industry.

And there's a spiritual side to their plans too. They mention that "God ordained the Sabbath as a day of rest" and think people should earn more if they work that day. Plus, they want to add work requirements for those receiving benefits from the Supplemental Nutrition Assistance Program.

Project 2025 has its members split when it comes to foreign trade. Peter Navarro is pushing for slapping higher, matching tariffs on goods from the European Union, China, and India to even out the trade scales. According to a Goldman Sachs analysis, these kind of protectionist moves could actually rake in enough money to pay for the tax cuts Project 2025 wants to make, and they might even boost the economy and help with inflation.

On the flip side, Kent Lassman from the Competitive Enterprise Institute is all about lowering tariffs. He thinks this would reduce prices for consumers and advocates for striking up more free-trade deals. Lassman points out that tariffs, whether from Trump or Biden's time, have not just hit the U.S. economy hard but have also strained our international relationships.

Even with these clashing opinions within Project 2025, the idea of using tariffs to economically distance from China and help American workers is a rare common ground found between Trump and Biden policies. This notion is also echoed in Project 2025's proposals.

Project 2025 Policy On Education And Research

Project 2025 is really concerned about what it describes as "woke propaganda" in public schools. Their solution? Cut back the federal government's involvement in education big time and bump up school choice and parental rights, arguing that education should mainly be a state matter.

To make this happen, they're proposing to scrap the Department of Education entirely and let states duck out of federal education programs and standards. They plan to move programs from the Individuals with Disabilities' Education Act (IDEA) over to the Department of Health and Human Services. The National Center for Education Statistics (NCES)? That would shift into the Census Bureau.

Project 2025 sees the federal role in education as largely keeping stats. They want to really dial back on federal civil rights enforcement in schools, handing it over to the Department of Justice, but limiting DOJ's actions to just litigation.

They're also against focusing on racial balance in school discipline measures like detentions and suspensions, putting student safety first. Plus, they're eyeing letting a huge $18 billion federal fund for low-income students run out, passing the buck to the states.

The project is all for using public money for school vouchers, even if parents choose private or religious schools, and they think stuff like free school lunches and the Head Start program should be cut, viewing education more as a private responsibility than a public one.

Lastly, Project 2025 wants any taxpayer-funded research to clearly align with the national interest and conservative values, which includes slashing funding for climatology research. They're painting a picture where personal choice and state control take precedence over federal oversight in schooling.

Project 2025 Policy on Expansion of the Presidential Powers

Kevin Roberts, the head of the Heritage Foundation, really doesn't like the idea of federal agencies or employees operating independently of the president. He thinks it's against the very principles of American democracy. Project 2025, the initiative he's championing, wants to bring the entire executive branch squarely under the president's control. This would mean doing away with the independence of some pretty major agencies like the Department of Justice, the FBI, the Federal Communications Commission, and the Federal Trade Commission.

The reasoning behind this aggressive push? It's based on a pretty extreme take on the unitary executive theory. This theory interprets the U.S. Constitution as putting all executive power in the hands of the president.

Project 2025 even goes as far as suggesting that all Department of State leaders should be booted out by January 20, 2025, and replaced with temporary leaders who don't need Senate confirmation. Kiron Skinner, who contributed to this part of Project 2025, argues that most State Department folks lean too left and need to be replaced by those who are firmly in the conservative camp.

Moreover, the project argues that selling military gear and ammo to other countries shouldn't need Congressional approval, unless it's guaranteed unanimous support from Congress.

Donald Trump, who is eyeing a return in the 2024 election, has often said that the Constitution gives him the freedom to do pretty much whatever he wants as president—a classic line from fans of the unitary executive theory. This idea has gained more traction within the Republican Party, especially since the events of 9/11.

According to a report from The Washington Post in November 2023, a big item on the agenda for a potential second Trump administration would be to use the military for domestic law enforcement and managing immigration under the Insurrection Act of 1807. Jeffrey Clark, who's involved with Project 2022 and used to work in Trump's Department of Justice, is leading this charge. Clark is also a senior fellow at the Center for Renewing America, one of the organizations linked to Project 2025.

The plan seems to include instructions for the Department of Justice to go after those Trump views as unfaithful or as political enemies. And just so you know, Clark himself isn't just talking policy from the sidelines — he's right in the thick of it as a co-defendant with Trump in the Georgia election racketeering case, and he's mentioned as an unnamed co-conspirator in another federal case accusing Trump of election obstruction, due to

Clark's actions at the DOJ during the last days of Trump's term.

After the story broke, a spokesperson from the Heritage Foundation, which spearheads Project 2025, claimed that the project doesn't involve using the Insurrection Act or targeting political opponents. Moreover, Media Matters highlighted that several partners associated with Project 2025 cheered on a 2020 Supreme Court decision, Trump v. United States, which apparently grants broad legal immunity for actions taken while fulfilling presidential duties.

Project 2025 Policy On Change Of Personnel

Project 2025 is aiming to shake things up in the federal civil service by switching tens of thousands of workers to political appointee status. The idea is to fill these slots with Trump loyalists prepared to push boundaries—bending or even breaking rules—to meet Trump's objectives. They've even put together a personnel database that's all about aligning with Trump's ideology. They screen potential recruits with a questionnaire to check how well they line up with the project's goals.

Trump has a history of ousting folks he saw as disloyal throughout his tenure, regardless of their political beliefs. Remember when he dismissed Attorney General William Barr? Towards the end of Trump's administration, White House personnel like James Bacon and John McEntee crafted a loyalty questionnaire for government job candidates. Both Bacon and McEntee moved over to the Project 2025 team in May 2023.

The plan also includes picking a White House Counsel who is fully on board with the president's "America First" agenda. And it plays well with Trump's ambition to fire more government employees than typically allowed. He had set up a system called Schedule F back in October 2020, which President Biden cancelled in January 2021. But Trump's hinted at bringing it back if he gets re-elected. The Heritage Foundation, the think tank behind Project 2025, is planning to stack their database with 20,000 names by the end of 2024 to help carry out these dismissals—a move one leader described as swinging a "wrecking ball" through the administrative state.

Now, there are currently about 4,000 political appointments in the government, but this number could change dramatically with the return of Schedule F. This could put many professional federal civil servants, who have served under both Democratic and Republican banners, at risk. Increasingly, some in the Republican Party view these experienced civil servants and their unions not as assets but as threats or entities to be managed, moving away from the traditional, non-partisan approach to staffing that's crucial for effective government operation.

Project 2021 is pushing Congress to make sure that 70% of federal contractors are American citizens, with an end goal of bumping that number up to 95%.

As of June 2024, the American Accountability Foundation, which is run by Tom Jones, a former aide to Republican senators, has been digging into the backgrounds of some top federal civil servants. They've got a side project called Project Sovereignty 2025, which got a cool $100,000 from the Heritage Foundation. The grand plan? They want to list 100 people on a website who they think might block Trump's agenda. When they handed over the grant in May 2024, Heritage said the research was all about cluing in Congress, any future conservative administration, and the public about what they call "anti-American bad actors" hidden within the government, to make sure something gets done about it.

This move, though, has some people feeling uneasy, drawing parallels to the McCarthy era—a time marked by accusations and blacklisting of supposed communists. The idea of singling out and targeting civil servants who might not be on board with Trump's agenda has sparked worries about a potential slide back to those kind of authoritarian and harsh measures.

Project 2025 Policy On Foreign Affairs

On the campaign trail, Trump hasn't really laid out what he plans to do about foreign policy if he gets a second term. However, Kiron Skinner, who penned the State Department section of Project 2025, sees China as a serious threat and isn't a fan of taking a soft approach with them. The preface of Project 2025 pulls no punches, claiming, "For 30 years, America's leaders in politics, economy, and culture have cozied up to Communist China and its genocidal regime, all while gutting America's industrial might."

According to Project 2025, the U.S. Agency for International Development (USAID) would see significant cutbacks, mainly because the Heritage Foundation is put off by what it calls the agency's focus on divisive political and cultural issues, like abortion, what they term as 'climate extremism,' 'gender radicalism,' and actions against supposed systemic racism.

The project wants to scrub the term "gender" from all USAID programs and documents completely. It also targets specific UN agencies to lose funding and suggests giving the president more authority over how the U.S. dishes out foreign aid. This aid wouldn't be used to help poorer nations with climate change impacts; instead, it'll support the interests of fossil fuel companies.

Project 2022 doesn't swing strongly towards interventionism or isolationism, but it makes clear that any foreign policy decisions should always put national interests first.

Project 2025 Nuclear Policy Proposition

Project 2025 has some pretty strong opinions on the U.S.'s nuclear stance. It suggests that the U.S. should only provide its nuclear protection, or 'nuclear umbrella,' to countries in the North Atlantic Treaty Organization (NATO). It also thinks these nations should bulk up their own conventional forces to keep Russian aggression in check. As of June 2024, every NATO country, except for Belgium, Canada, Croatia, Italy, Luxembourg, Portugal, Slovenia, and Spain, has already been spending at least 2% of their GDP on defense. Iceland, by the way, doesn't have a military.

The Bulletin of the Atomic Scientists has had a lot to say about Project 2025's nuclear ideas, describing them as "the most dramatic buildup of nuclear weapons since the Reagan era," hinting at the start of a new global nuclear arms race. The plan suggests ramping up nuclear weapon development and production, even prioritizing it above other security efforts, and dismissing any Congressional attempts to find more cost-effective solutions. It even talks about stacking up nuclear weapons beyond treaty limits, shrugging off current arms control treaties, beefing up the National Nuclear Security Administration (NNSA), and getting ready to test new nukes against the Comprehensive Nuclear Test Ban Treaty. There's also a push to speed up all missile defense programs.

Specifically, Project 2025 outlines a pretty full-on nuclear strategy. The plan kicks off with a post-inauguration speech aimed at convincing Americans that nuclear arms are key to their freedom and prosperity. Next steps include building new and modernized warheads, deploying a new nuclear-armed sea-launched cruise missile, setting up advanced defense systems like directed-energy and space-based weapons, and defending against cruise missiles targeting the homeland. They also want to load up each Minuteman III ICBM and its future Sentinel replacement with multiple warheads by 2026, arm Army ground-launched missiles with nukes, attach nuclear options to hypersonic missile systems, explore a road-mobile ICBM launcher for the Air Force, and ramp up the placement of nuclear bombs in Europe and Asia. The NNSA would also shift to a wartime footing, supported by directing the NNSA for frequent briefings to the Oval Office, submitting independent budget requests separate from the Energy Department, and asking the Office of Management and Budget to push through a supplemental budget request to Congress.

Project 2025 Policy On Healthcare And Public Health

Project 2025 has a lot to say about the Biden administration, accusing it of weakening the traditional nuclear family structure. Their plan? To overhaul the Department of Health and Human Services (DHHS) to promote this sort of family setup again. They also want to stop Medicare from negotiating drug prices and push the Medicare Advantage program, which is all about private insurance plans.

When it comes to healthcare, the project has some controversial ideas, like denying gender-affirming care to transgender individuals and getting rid of insurance coverage for the morning-after-pill Ella which is currently part of Obamacare. And there's more: they're looking to slash Medicaid funding in several ways, such as capping the federal funds it can receive, setting limits on lifetime benefits per capita, and letting states enforce tougher work requirements for those who benefit from this program.

They also want to limit states' use of provider taxes, scrap preexisting federal beneficiary protections, ramp up eligibility and asset checks to make getting and renewing Medicaid harder, potentially turn Medicaid into a voucher system, and get rid of federal oversight over state Medicaid programs.

But wait—there's even a plan for the National Institutes of Health (NIH). Project 2025 wants to make it easier to fire NIH employees and ditch their Diversity, Equity, and Inclusion (DEI) programs. They're branding the NIH as corrupt and politically biased.

Lastly, they're pointing fingers at social media giants like Facebook, Instagram, Twitter, and TikTok, blaming them for endangering the mental health and social connections of young Americans by fostering an addictive digital environment.

Project 2025's stance is pretty clear: federal policies should not allow this to continue.

Project 2025 Policy On The Reform Of Immigration

In Project 2025, the idea is to replace the Department of Homeland Security (DHS) with a new immigration agency. This agency would bring together various existing organizations like Customs and Border Protection (CBP), the Transportation Security Administration (TSA), Immigration and Customs Enforcement (ICE), and the U.S. Citizenship and Immigration Services (USCIS). Some tasks may also be privatized. The plan includes reducing the admission of refugees and increasing processing fees for asylum seekers to generate more funds. Immigrants who want their applications expedited would have to pay even more.

Former President Trump has said that if he were reelected, he would carry out the largest domestic deportation operation in American history. The Heritage Foundation stated that Project 2025 involves arresting, detaining, and removing immigration violators anywhere in the United States. Stephen Miller, a key figure in shaping immigration policy during the Trump presidency, is heavily involved in Project 2025 and could potentially serve a senior role in a second Trump administration. Miller has outlined plans for a deportation operation that would involve the National Guard and other law enforcement agencies, targeting illegal immigrants in large-scale raids and holding them in internment camps before deportation.

There is also talk of rounding up homeless people in Democratic-led cities and detaining them. Funding for the border wall would also be increased.

Finally, Project 2025 encourages the president to withhold federal disaster relief funds from state or local governments that refuse to cooperate with federal immigration laws, such as withholding information from law enforcement.

Project 2025 Policy On Personal Identity

In Project 2025, they strongly oppose what they refer to as "radical gender ideology" and believe that the government should stick to a definition of marriage and family that aligns with biblical teachings and social science research. To bring about this vision, they propose putting an end to same-sex marriage and removing protections against discrimination based on sexual or gender identity.

They also want to get rid of diversity, equity, and inclusion (DEI) initiatives, which they label as "state-sanctioned racism," from federal laws. They even suggest that federal employees who have participated in DEI programs or initiatives related to critical race theory could face potential dismissal. Furthermore, they want public school teachers to obtain written permission from parents before using transgender students' preferred pronouns.

Supporters of Project 2025 also aim to reverse what they see as a shift towards DEI policies in the private sector and advocate for more "race-neutral" regulations. This is part of a larger backlash against DEI initiatives that gained momentum in the early 2020s.

The proposal goes further by recommending the disbandment of the White House's Gender Policy Council. They also suggest prohibiting government agencies from implementing quotas or collecting statistics on gender, race, or ethnicity. Jonathan Berry, a contributor to the project, explains that the aim is to move towards colorblindness and ensure that laws and policies treat people as whole individuals rather than reducing them to categories, particularly regarding race. Additionally, the plan calls for conservative principles to guide the reform of the U.S. Census Bureau.

Project 2025 Policy On Law Enforcement

According to Project 2025, the Department of Justice (DOJ) has become a bloated bureaucracy that is overly focused on pushing a liberal agenda. They believe that the DOJ has lost the trust of the American people, especially due to its involvement in investigating alleged Trump-Russia collusion. The proposal puts forth the idea of a thorough reform of the DOJ and increased oversight from the White House. They even suggest that the director of the Federal Bureau of Investigation (FBI) should be directly answerable to the president.

In line with the recommendations of Project 2025, a reformed DOJ would aim to combat what they see as "affirmative discrimination" or "anti-white racism," invoking the Civil Rights Act of 1964. Former Trump DOJ official Gene Hamilton argues that prioritizing certain segments of society infringes on the rights of others and violates existing federal laws. Accordingly, the DOJ's Civil Rights Division would prosecute any state or local governments, educational institutions, corporations, or other private employers with diversity, equity, and inclusion (DEI) or affirmative action programs.

The plan also proposes scaling back the use of legal settlements known as "consent decrees" between the DOJ and local police departments. Additionally, it suggests that if the FBI and another federal agency, like the Drug Enforcement Administration (DEA), have overlapping responsibilities, the latter should take the lead, allowing the FBI to focus on other serious crimes and threats to national security.

Project 2025 recognizes the sensitivity surrounding capital punishment but still promotes its use for dealing with what they perceive as an ongoing crime wave and particularly severe crimes like pedophilia, until Congress decides otherwise.

Lastly, echoing former President Trump, Project 2025 contends that the District of Columbia is plagued by crime. As a solution, they propose granting the Uniformed Division of the Secret Service the authority to enforce the law beyond just the immediate area around the White House.

Project 2025 Policy On National Security

In Project 2025, they propose some changes for the Pentagon. Firstly, they want the elimination of diversity, equity, and inclusion (DEI) programs within the Department of Defense. Additionally, they insist on reinstating all service members who were discharged for refusing to receive the COVID-19 vaccine.

Another aspect of Project 2025 is that it argues against considering climate change as a factor in assessing national security threats. They believe that the United States Armed Forces should not take this into account.

The project highlights China as the primary threat to U.S. national security. It raises concerns about China's influence over American society. They recommend banning TikTok, which they accuse of engaging in espionage. They also propose the closure of Confucius Institutes, which they claim undermine American higher education.

Intellectual property theft by China is another issue raised by the project, as well as allegations that major technology companies are working to undermine the United States on behalf of the Chinese Communist Party. Furthermore, Project 2025 suggests that American pension funds should avoid investing in China and proposes restrictions or denials of permission for American companies seeking to invest in sensitive sectors in China.

Project 2025 Policy On Pornography

In Project 2025, Kevin Roberts, in the foreword of the mandate, expresses strong concerns about the negative effects of pornography. He argues that it promotes sexual deviance, the sexualization of children, and the exploitation of women. Roberts goes as far as suggesting that pornography should be banned, asserting that it is not protected by the First Amendment of the United States Constitution.

He even recommends the criminal prosecution of individuals and companies involved in producing pornography, comparing it to addictive drugs. However, it's worth noting that the Supreme Court has previously ruled against attempts to ban pornography based on First Amendment grounds.

During his 2016 presidential campaign, when Donald Trump received the Republican Party nomination, he signed a pledge to investigate the impact of internet pornography on public health, youth, families, and American culture.

However, he did not fulfill this promise. Despite allegations of affairs involving adult-film star Stormy Daniels and Playboy model Karen McDougal in 2006, Kevin Roberts, in his response to CNN, showed little concern. He believed that even with imperfections, Trump can still be a powerful messenger and that embracing those imperfections may even strengthen his message overall.

Project 2025 Policy On Reproduction

In Project 2025, they firmly believe that life begins at conception. They argue for the Department of Health and Human Services (HHS) to be renamed the "Department of Life," a term previously used by former Trump HHS Secretary Alex Azar in 2020, expressing pride in their administration's strong pro-life stance. The goal of Project 2025 is to reshape HHS policies by explicitly rejecting the notion that abortion is healthcare and restoring the department's mission statement to include the promotion of health and well-being for all Americans "from conception to natural death."

Following the Supreme Court's Dobbs v. Jackson Women's Health Organization ruling in 2022, which removed the federal constitutional right to abortion, Project 2025 now urges the next president to implement the most extensive protections for the unborn that Congress will support.

Roger Severino, Vice President of Domestic Policy at the Heritage Foundation, stated that Project 2025 is actively working on executive orders and regulations to reverse Biden-era abortion policies and institutionalize the post-Dobbs environment. This involves replacing the Reproductive Healthcare Access Task Force with a dedicated "pro-life" agency focused on promoting the life and health of both women and their unborn children. Project 2025 also opposes initiatives it views as subsidizing single parenthood.

Additionally, they encourage the next administration to rescind specific provisions of the Family Planning Services and Population Research Act of 1970 (Title X of the Public Health Service Act), which provides reproductive healthcare services, and require participating clinics to emphasize the importance of marriage to potential parents.

In the manifesto of the project, Severino argues that the Food and Drug Administration should reassess and withdraw its initial approval of mifepristone and misoprostol, commonly known as abortion pills. He also suggests that the Centers for Disease Control and Prevention should update its messaging on the effectiveness of modern fertility awareness-based methods, including smartphone applications that track a woman's menstrual cycle.

Severino further recommends that every state should be required by the Department of Health and Human Services to report precise information on the number of abortions performed within their borders, including the gestational age of the child, the reasons for the abortion, the mother's state of residence, and the method used.

Project 2025 also aims to reinstate Trump-era religious and moral exemptions to contraceptive requirements under the Affordable Care Act. This includes emergency contraception, which they consider to be an abortifacient. They also seek to defund Planned Parenthood and remove protection for medical records related to abortions from criminal investigations if the records cross state lines. Project 2025 contributor Emma Waters emphasizes that their policy recommendations are intended to provide medical safeguards for women rather than imposing restrictions. She also advocates for the National Institutes of Health to investigate the long-term effects of contraception.

In the section concerning the Department of Justice, project contributor Gene Hamilton calls for enforcement of federal law against using the U.S.

Postal Service to transport abortion-inducing medicines.

The project aims to revive provisions of the Comstock Act from the 1870s, which banned the delivery of any item related to abortion by mail. This would enable the criminal prosecution of both senders and receivers of abortion pills. Although the project does not explicitly advocate for the prohibition of abortion, some legal experts and abortion rights advocates believe that implementing the project's plan could effectively create a de facto national abortion ban by limiting access to medical equipment used in surgical abortions.

When it comes to abortion, it's important to note that Trump has not committed to a federal ban on abortion. He understands that the majority of public opinion is against such a step.

Regarding preventing teenage pregnancy, Project 2025 recommends that the federal government moves away from what they see as promoting abortion and high-risk sexual behaviors among adolescents. They also propose limiting the role of the Department of Health and Human Services in shaping sex education, arguing that it would create a monopoly.

In simpler terms, the project aims to decrease the government's involvement in promoting abortion and comprehensive sex education for teenagers. Instead, they support an approach they believe would be more effective in preventing teenage pregnancies. However, it's important to note that the project does not explicitly call for a nationwide ban on abortion. They recognize the political challenges and widespread opposition such a measure would face.

Project 2025 Policy On Transportation

In Project 2025, they propose scaling back the Bipartisan Infrastructure Law of 2021, which provides funding for decarbonizing transportation infrastructure. They also express a negative stance towards the Federal Transit Administration (FTA), calling it a waste of money, and recommend reducing federal funding for transit agencies nationwide through the Capital Investment Grants (CIG) program.

Furthermore, they suggest that the FTA should conduct rigorous cost-benefit analyses on projects, even though the agency already undergoes a thorough review process before allocating funds.

Simply put, Project 2025 aims to reduce the level of federal investment in sustainable transportation infrastructure and public transit systems. Their argument is based on the belief that the current funding mechanisms and oversight by agencies are inefficient or unnecessary. They advocate for a more limited government role in promoting the use of clean transportation and expanding public transit options throughout the country.

Major Reactions To Project 2025

Project 2025 has faced several backlashes and criticisms from the public. In this section we will review some of the reactions and responses to this project.

Scholar Ruth Ben-Ghiat from New York University argues that Project 2025 is a plan to establish authoritarian rule in the United States, cleverly disguised under a seemingly neutral name. According to Ben-Ghiat, the project aims to dismantle federal departments and agencies in order to systematically undermine the legal and governance structures of liberal democracy.

The ultimate goal is to replace these structures with new bureaucracies staffed by politically aligned individuals who would help uphold autocratic rule. Ben-Ghiat also explains that the project's adoption of civil rights rhetoric for white Christians is a Trumpist tactic to undermine the cause of racial equality. It seeks to prioritize Christian nationalism as a central objective of domestic policy. Many key figures in Project 2025, such as Russ Vought and Michael Flynn, are proponents of eliminating the separation of church and state. They justify this as part of a "spiritual war" and a counterrevolutionary strategy.

According to Ben-Ghiat, figures like Bannon, Roberts, and Stephen Miller, who are associated with American fascism, believe that an autocratic counterrevolution is the only viable path for their far-right ideologies due to the unpopularity of their positions, particularly on issues like abortion, and the legal challenges faced by their leader.

Political scientist Rachel Beatty Riedl from Cornell University shares concerns about Project 2025, seeing it as an alarming concentration of executive power and a form of democratic retrogression involving institutional changes implemented by elected leaders. While examples of such backsliding can be found in countries like Hungary, Nicaragua, and Turkey, Riedl points out that it is a relatively new phenomenon in the United States. If implemented, Riedl warns that Project 2025 would significantly diminish the ability of American citizens to participate in public life based on the core principles of liberty, freedom, and representation that define a democracy.

According to Donald B. Ayer, a former deputy attorney general under George H.W. Bush, Project 2025 seems to be centered around providing Donald Trump with the tools to act as a dictator. Ayer believes that the project's goal is to completely dismantle the checks and balances built into the U.S. system, indicating Trump's intent to undermine the rule of law. Ayer issued a warning that if the reports about Project 2025 are accurate, and if Trump were to be reelected and implement some of these ideas, then the safety of every person in the country would be at risk.

Michael Bromwich, who served as the Justice Department's inspector general in the late 1990s, expressed concern about the plans being developed by members of what he refers to as Trump's "cult."

He asserts that these plans aim to transform the Department of Justice (DOJ) and the Federal Bureau of Investigation (FBI) into instruments of revenge. Bromwich believes that anyone who values the rule of law should be disturbed by these developments. He states that Trump and right-wing media have successfully fostered the belief that the current DOJ is highly political, and this narrative has gained traction. Bromwich considers the attempts to undermine the DOJ and the FBI as some of the most harmful campaigns conducted by Trump and his supporters.

Max Stier from the Partnership for Public Service, along with others, have raised concerns about Project 2025 potentially resurrecting an old spoils-and-patronage system in American politics where government jobs are handed out based on loyalty to a party or elected official rather than on merit. They worry that this could undermine the merit-based principles established by the Pendleton Act of 1883. Steve Bannon, former senior advisor to the Trump campaign and presidency, has supported this plan on his War Room podcast, hosting discussions with Jeffrey Clark and other project contributors.

Donald Moynihan, a public policy professor at Georgetown University, suggests that under Project 2025, Schedule F appointees could be required to pledge loyalty to the president, which would conflict with their constitutional obligation to uphold loyalty to the U.S. Constitution.

Political scientist Francis Fukuyama believes that while the federal bureaucracy is in need of reform, the implementation of Schedule F would dangerously compromise the functioning of the government.

Several commentators, including Spencer Ackerman, John Nichols from The Nation, and Chauncey DeVega from Salon.com, have characterized Project 2025 as a scheme to install Trump as a dictator. They warn of the potential for Trump to prosecute and imprison his adversaries or even subvert American democracy altogether. In The Atlantic, long-time Republican academic Tom Nichols writes that Trump is not bluffing about his intentions to imprison his opponents and suppress the rights of American citizens, even through force if necessary.

Calling attention to Project 2025 in Mother Jones, David Corn, Washington bureau chief, describes it as a right-wing infrastructure openly strategizing to undermine the checks and balances enshrined in our constitutional order, while concentrating unprecedented power in the presidency. Corn argues that if successful and combined with a Trump or other GOP victory in 2024, this project could lead the nation down a path towards autocracy.

Peter M. Shane, a law professor specializing in the rule of law and separation of powers, discussed the perspective of Russell Vought, former director of the Office of Management and Budget. Vought expressed impatience with conservative lawyers in the first Trump administration who hesitated to carry out Trump's orders without question.

He criticized the cautiousness of traditional conservative lawyers, stating that "The Federalist Society doesn't know what time it is," as reported by The New York Times. In regard to making the Justice Department a tool for political retribution, Vought told The Washington Post that the norm of independence, maintained by presidents and attorneys general of both parties since Watergate, could be discarded. Vought suggested that a mindset shift was needed, with an attorney general and White House Counsel's Office that do not see themselves as protecting the department from the president.

Jeff Sharlet, a professor at Dartmouth College, who has engaged with Trump supporters, acknowledged in his book from 2023, The Undertow: Scenes from a Slow Civil War, that his initial objections to describe militant Trumpism as fascist have diminished.

Sharlet argues that Project 2025 is influenced by the New Apostolic Reformation, an evangelical and charismatic movement aligned with Trump that is experiencing rapid growth. He posits that the project's first mandate to "restore the family as the centerpiece of American life and protect our children" carries coded messaging related to white supremacist ideologies and echoes slogans like the "14 words."

Responding to criticism of the project, the Heritage Foundation released a 13-page document in April

2024 titled "5 Reasons Leftists HATE Project ⌐

In this document, they reiterated many of the project's stated objectives. They also claimed that the "radical Left" is hostile towards families and aims to replace them with the state, that climate change is used by leftist elites as a tool to manipulate and control Americans, and that the left seeks to turn the country into a Soviet Union, North Korea, or Cuba. The document also called for the elimination of "woke propaganda" at all levels of government.

Considering the project's likely support base, it is expected to have significant backing from individuals dissatisfied with Washington or in favor of specific right-wing and conservative policy proposals.

Back in June 2024, Democratic Congressman Jared Huffman made an announcement about the creation of The Stop Project 2025 Task Force. He emphasized the urgency of the situation, comparing the potential impact of the project to a sudden and overwhelming military attack, stating that if we wait until it happens to react, it will be too late. Huffman stressed the importance of being aware of it well in advance and taking proactive measures to prepare. In 2023, Michael Hirsh wrote that much of Project 2025's agenda is unlikely to materialize.

He cited criticism from conservative scholars and government experts, who regarded the plans to reform the federal bureaucracy as overly simplistic and unrealistic, potentially leading to greater incompetence, chaos, and amateurism within the federal government.

Criticism from LGBTQ+ writers and journalists has been directed towards Project 2025 for its intention to remove protections for LGBTQ+ individuals and its determination to outlaw pornography by associating it with the "propagation of transgender ideology and sexualization of children." Brynn Tannehill, writing for Dame magazine, argued that the project prioritizes eradicating LGBTQ+ people from public life, highlighting passages from the plan that link pornography to transgender ideology. This connection has been seen as part of a larger wave of anti-transgender attacks in 2023.

Guthrie Graves-Fitzsimmons, the author of Just Faith: Reclaiming Progressive Christianity, criticized Project 2025 in an article on MSNBC, specifically calling out its appeal to Christian nationalism. Graves-Fitzsimmons highlighted Severino's chapter on the U.S. Department of Health and Human Services, which opposes the Respect for Marriage Act—a significant law that repealed the Defense of Marriage Act, officially recognizing same-sex and interracial marriages at the federal level.

Just before Biden's presidential debate with Trump on June 27, 2024, the Biden campaign launched a website critical of Project 2025.

In an article for the libertarian magazine Reason, Steven Greenhut voiced his concerns about Project

2025, criticizing it for increasing government power and the potential risks of authoritarianism and abuse that come with centralizing executive control in the President.

The project has employed strong, warlike language and apocalyptic rhetoric when describing its "battle plan" to regain control of the government. Some observers have interpreted this language as potentially indicating a threat of political violence.

On July 5, 2024, Trump publicly distanced himself from Project 2025 in a statement on his platform, Truth Social. He claimed to have no knowledge of the project, expressing disagreement with some of its ideas, describing them as absurd and terrible. He wished them luck but made it clear that he had no association with them.

Conclusion

Project 2025 is essentially a bold and ambitious plan to transform America into a Christian nationalist state guided by conservative principles. Led by the Heritage Foundation and backed by over 100 right-wing groups, this extensive 920-page document lays out a comprehensive roadmap for reshaping the federal government based on far-right ideals. It covers a wide range of objectives, from restoring traditional family values to dismantling the administrative state, defending national sovereignty, and securing individual rights through a conservative Christian lens.

The project proposes significant overhauls across government agencies to advance its agenda on contentious issues like abortion, LGBTQ+ rights, climate policy, immigration, and more. With a 180-day playbook at its disposal, Project 2025 aims to swiftly put its vision into action should a conservative president take office in 2025. This would involve purging the federal workforce of those whose views don't align with the project's ideology while appointing like-minded individuals at every level of government.

As the outcome of the 2024 election hangs in the balance, Project 2025 serves as a stark reminder of the aspirations of the radical conservative movement to fundamentally reshape American democracy and society. Its success would pose a significant setback for civil rights, social progress, and the preservation of democratic norms in the United States.

About The Author

JR Grant likes explaining political concepts in simple terms for everyone to understand.

As an advocate for democracy and social progress, Grant brings a vital voice to the conversation on pressing issues. Through his writing, he seeks to ignite dialogue and inspire readers to question the world around them.

Made in the USA
Middletown, DE
10 October 2024